Polish Recipes Cookbook

By Billie A Williams

Billie A Williams

www.billieawilliams.co
m

All Rights Reserved

Dedication

This book is dedicated to cultural diversity wherever it is found. We have so much to share and in the sharing we grow when we learn from each other. Food is the greatest equalizer of all. With that said I hope you will enjoy this short cookbook and will share the fruits of your labor with everyone. Invite them to your table to share your harvest or your meager fare. My mother always made room for one more mouth at our table and gladly fed our friends or anyone who was around at meal time. She was the magician of extending any meal to include however many showed up. We had a very happy family. Share your blessing and you will too.

POLISH TRADITIONAL RECIPES

TABLE OF CONTENTS

CHRISTMAS GINGER BREAD

Ginger Bread traditional Polish Gingerbread that is, was often part of the dowry of Polish maidens. Unbaked the dough must mature not less than 2 weeks in a cool place (the lowest shelf of your refrigerator or, in a cool cellar – which is better, according to the source.)

Gradually heat almost to the boiling point:
1 pound of real honey
2 cups of sugar
10 ounces of Lard or butter

Cool:

Add to cooled mixture: (Kneading with hands as mixture thickens with each addition)
2 pounds wheat flour
3 whole eggs
3 level teaspoons baking soda dissolved in ½ cup of cold milk
½ teaspoon salt
½ teaspoon each cinnamon, cloves, ginger, cardamom (adjusting the amount of your favorite up and less for those not as well liked – 1 ½ to 2 ½ teaspoons total)

Add :
A handful of crushed nuts
3 tablespoons finely chopped, candied orange peel

Knead dough thoroughly, shape into a ball and place in a crock covered with a clean linen cloth in a cool place so it can mature slowly.

TO BAKE: Divide mature dough into 2 – 3 parts after rolling it out, bake on a metal cookie sheet.
350 degree oven for 10 – 12 minutes check for doneness with tooth pick – if it comes out clean it's done.
(Note: after baking they become hard, but in 2 or 3 days they'll become crumbly and almost melt in your mouth.)

CHRISTMAS EVE BORSCH

How to sour beet juice:
Carefully wash 3 pounds of beets
Peel and thinly slice
Place in a glass jar and cover completely with barely lukewarm water.
Place a slice of wheat bread on top.
Cover jar with gauze and place in the warmest place in the kitchen

After 4 or 5 days, carefully remove foam from the surface and pour the clear, ruby-red soured juice into clean bottles. (In tightly corked bottles, in a cool place, they can be stored for months)

Vegetable Stock:
Celeriac & parsley root
Carrots
Leek
1 onion
4 red beets, peeled and thinly sliced
10 grains of black pepper
2 grains pimento (allspice)
A small piece of bay leaf

In a separate pot: cook 2 – 3 ounces of dried mushrooms (boletus) in 2 cups water.
Pour both stocks through a sieve and mix together.

Add: ¾ pints of prepared beet juice to 2 ½ pints stock
Heat to boiling point, enhance with a glass of dry red wine or lemon juice. About 15 minutes before serving add a crushed garlic clove. Uszka (ravioli) 6 – 8 for each person,

are traditionally added...place the Uszka in a soup tureen and cover with hot borsch.

Uszka for Christmas Eve Borsch

DOUGH: Knead 6 ounces of flour with 1 whole egg and a pinch of salt. The dough should be stiffer than for noodles. If it is too stiff, add a little lukewarm water while kneading.

Roll the well kneaded dough out thinly and cut into small squares (1 ½ x 1 ½ inches or slightly smaller) The greater the skill of the cook, the small the Uszka. Place some farce on each square, fold over diagonally, press firmly together, first around the edge, then the two opposite corners of the triangle. Throw the Uszka into salted boiling water. They are ready when they come up to the surface.

FARCE: Dice very finely the cooked mushrooms from which the stock has been added to the borsch. Fry in butter with a small, finely chopped onion, then blend thoroughly with 1 tablespoon bread crumbs and 1 whole raw egg. Add salt and pepper to taste.

Christmas Eve Mushroom Soup

Pour 3 12 pints lukewarm water over 2 – 3 ounces of dried *boletus mushrooms*, cook covered over low heat.

When softened add: celeriac and parsley root, carrots, leeks, onion, 10 grains black pepper and cook for 25 – 30 minutes.

Strain soup through a fine sieve, salt to taste and add lemon juice if desired.

Add cooked mushroom caps sliced into thin strips and cooked Lazanki [recipe follows on next page] (a kind of noodle) and heat through.

*More about the Boletus Mushroom

This recipe calls for Boletus mushrooms, now these mushrooms can be obtained from Spain, handpicked from the local villagers. From the forests near Zamora, these giant mushrooms are gathered by hand. They have been prized for centuries for their aromatic flavor and meaty texture. They are famous across Europe as the king of mushrooms.

Serve them chopped and added to pasta or rice, or heated and served as a warm tapa.

Faundez is a tiny company in the village of Rabanales, where cows still roam the streets and everyone is like family. Each year during the season, members of all of the surrounding villages will go to their favorite mushroom gathering spot in the forest and harvest these precious mushrooms. And each night the owner of the company drives his van from house to house purchasing their prize mushrooms.

He then drives them back to his surprisingly modern facility across the street from his home. There his team cleans and prepares the mushrooms using just olive oil and salt. They are then jarred and shared with the greater world.

This innovative company has helped pull this tiny town forward from a subsistence level to a prosperous village. We were proudly shown the town museum including rough linen clothing and tools of drudgery that were used only a generation ago. It was an amazing site, and we hope our support will contribute to the villagers' new-found vitality.

La Tienda, The Best of Spain with offices in Williamsburg, Virginia

Lazanki

Ingredients

- 1 medium head cabbage, sliced
- 1 (8 ounce) package uncooked spaghetti
- 1 tablespoon vegetable oil
- 2 large onions, sliced
- salt and pepper to taste
- 2 tablespoons soy sauce

Directions

1. Preheat oven to 450 degrees F (230 degrees C).
2. Bring a large pot of salted water to a boil. Add cabbage and cook until tender, about 15 minutes; drain.
3. Meanwhile, bring a large pot of lightly salted water to a boil. Add pasta and cook for 8 to 10 minutes or until al dente; drain.
4. While the pasta and cabbage are cooking, heat oil in a large skillet over medium heat. Saute onions until tender.
5. Combine cabbage, pasta, onions, salt, pepper and soy sauce; mix well and transfer to a 9x13 inch casserole dish.
6. Bake in preheated oven for 30 minutes.

FRIED CARP

Clean and cut into portions, slat and let rest for 30 minutes.

Dredge each portion with flour, dip in lightly beaten egg and sprinkle with bread crumbs.

Fry in butter over moderate heat until golden brown.

Horseradish is served with fried carp or cabbage with mushrooms.

BOILED PIKE PERCH

2 lbs scaled and cleaned Pike Perch, salt.

Prepare light vegetable stock of celeriac and parsley root, carrots, leeks, a large onion and a few grains of black pepper, a small piece of bay leaf.

Place whole fish in a shallow pan and cover with cold vegetable stock from above. Slowly bring fish to a boil and simmer covered, over low heat, 15 – 20 minutes. Leave fish in stock and keep warm.

In saucepan melt 2 ounces of butter and add 3 finely chopped hard-boiled eggs and a tablespoon of minced parsley. Heat well, do not fry.

Carefully place hot fish on a warmed platter, sprinkle evenly with juice of ½ lemon and add hot mixture of butter, eggs, parsley.

CABBAGE WITH MUSHROOMS AND NUT CROQUETTES

Pour 2 cups water over 2 pounds of sauerkraut, cook until tender.

In a separate pan: cook 2 – 3 ounces dried mushrooms in a small amount of water until tender.

Slice cooked mushroom into think strips and add to cabbage with stock.

Season cabbage with a light roux made of 2 tablespoons butter, 1 tablespoon flour, also add I large, finely chopped onion that has been fried to a golden brown.

Add salt and pepper to taste cook until thick.

CROQUETTES: Mash 12 ounces freshly cooked hot potatoes,

Add:
4 ounces ground walnuts
1 whole egg
1 heaping teaspoon bread crumbs
1 tablespoon very finely minced parsley.
Salt to taste

Mix by hand, shape into small croquettes. Coat in egg and bread crumbs then fry in butter to golden brown.
Arrange on cabbage and serve immediately.

JUNIPER SAUCE
(This is Leona Augustine's favorite reminder of home)
Chop left over game into very small pieces to make 2
tablespoons
Add:
2 ounces smoked bacon
1 finally chopped onion
1 Tablespoon dried juniper berries
½ finely chopped medium carrot
¼ finely chopped celeriac

Lightly brown 1 ounce flour in 1 ounce butter and add
vegetable with juniper, cook and rub through a sieve.

Add: ½ cup of dry white wine, and salt to taste.
A teaspoon of good tomato paste may also be added to
enliven the flavor.

Widely used in polish cooking, added to roast game,
pork and lamb and to pates that are served hot.

POLISH KRUPNIK (Barley Soup)

Pour 3 ½ pints water over 1 pound cubed beef and 1 pound of beef soup bones. Cook over low heat for 1 hour.

Add:
Carrots
Parsley
Celeriac root
Leek and onion
4 small dried mushrooms
When meat is tender, strain

Cut meat into cubes, vegetables and mushrooms into thin strips.

Cook ¾ pint of the cooked broth, salted to taste, with 4 – 6 ounces pearl barley. When cooked, Add 1 tablespoon butter and mix with a wooden spoon until it turns white.

Add to the remaining broth with 3 diced cubed potatoes. Cook 15 – 20 minutes more.

Add diced meat, sliced mushrooms and vegetables and salt to taste. Sprinkle with minced parsley before serving.

[A pint equals 4 cups]

BEER SOUP WITH EGG YOLKS

[This soup found on Breakfast tables, before coffee became
popular]

Bring to boil, 1 1/3 pints light beer and ¾ pint water, 2 – 3
cloves and a piece of stick cinnamon. When soup is hot
add 4 slightly beaten egg yolks to which 3-4 ounces of
sugar have been added.

Add croutons made of pieces of bread fried golden born in
1 tablespoon of butter.

WINE SOUP WITH SPICES
[For the Ladies]

In enameled sauce pan, heat thoroughly ¾ pint dry red wine with ¾ pint of water, 3 cloves, a piece of cinnamon, a slice of lemon or orange peel and 4 ounces of sugar.

Just before serving add ¼ pint sweet cream to the soup.

Billie A Williams

www.billieawilliams.co
m
SOURCES:

Old Polish Traditions, in the Kitchen and at the Table by
Maria Lemnis and Henryk Vitry

Hippocrene Books (seventh printing 2010) Warsaw:
Interpress 1981
ISBN 978-0-7818-0488-2
ISBN o-7818-0488-4

This beautiful book briefly outlines the history of Polish
culinary custom and traditions as well as hospitality,
holiday traditions and traditional family fair. These are a
few recipes from that collection, but there is so much
more you are encouraged to buy the book and explore on
your own.

Boletus Mushrooms – Google Search - La Tienda, The Best
of Spain with offices in Williamsburg, Virginia

Lazanki Noodles: Google Search – Kraft Recipes

Other Works From The Pen Of
Billie A. Williams

Death by Candlelight October 2002

Family dynamics have a far reaching affect. The abused wife is ready to resort to an elaborate scheme and at the same time the sister, Ruth Ord, has her own designs. When the two women's paths cross, their plans are altered. But Randolph Ord III still turns up dead.

It is now up to detective Sandy March to find the real killer. Is his judgment being compromised by the growing attraction he feels toward the newly widowed Danielle Ord? Both women have motive and opportunity; but a third figure emerges with ties to organized crime.

Candlelight and Shadows January 2005

The future looks bleak; Danielle's husband murdered; heart trouble in her premature infant son, David, forces her to turn to the senior Ord's for financial help. A revengeful serial killer stalks, threatens Danielle, and murders anyone connected to the Ord's; then kidnaps the infant. Can Detective March save the people he loves?

Skull Music June 2005

Revenge produces a serial killer; research produces a cover for terrorist activities. Reporter (CHARLIE WOLFE) unravels the webs of each while she battles her attraction to lawyer DAVID ASHBECK. Will she find the serial killer, stop the terrorists and reconcile her impression of lawyers with David before she loses her life or him?

Ghost Music of Vaudeville April 2008

Damien Callistrari orders his henchmen to remove the tenants of the old Keith Theatre Building.. Did he mean at any price, including kidnapping, arson, or murder? The residents refuse to be bought out. Will Charlie be able to save the theatre and her friends when money speaks louder than ethics?

When Damien's son falls in love with Charlie Wolfe, Reporter for the Ironwood Daily Globe, all bets are off. He is suddenly confronted with the evil man his father has become. Can Roberto stop Damien from destroying the theater, more importantly the lives so wrapped up in the memories of the Vaudeville shows that still haunt the walls of the beloved Keith Theatre —what will be the cost?

Knapsack Secrets May 2008
In a few days time, Audrey Fleta Hroc's 20 year career ends in disgrace, an 18 year marriage ends in divorce, and the home she has cherished for all those years burns down with her possessions in it, nearly taking he with it. Sometimes she wishes it had. Audrey Fleta Hroc alone, jobless and homeless asked, "Can it get any worse?" It does, much worse.

Cold Water July 2012 Young Adult Zip's Story (from Knapsack Secrets)

Bullied, homeless, alone, wait it-- gets worse...Zip's skateboard represents survival and freedom, until he finds those who need his help, and maybe his treasured skateboard, worse.

Small Town Secrets January 2008

Someone is bent on burning down Nettlesville, Wisconsin—a small, rural remote, community—one building at a time. The cause is arson, but with no suspect, no person of interest, Olga Corn Editor in Chief, owner of The Daily Nettle Newspaper, stirs the pot of unrest blaming Chaneeta, Town Chairperson, for allowing the town Constable to go on a month long vacation leaving the town under the protection of his female deputy Taaktu Tewsday.

A new deputy, also a new arrival in town, Hope Morgan Anderson, has ties to NYPD (The New York Police Department) will she be enough to assist Taaktu. At this point, no one knows that the new arrival is the illegitimate child of Chaneeta Morgan Bailey. No one accept Olga Corn, that is, who discovered the skeleton in Chaneeta's past that included this child,(now a woman), and an arrest on Chaneeta's record for armed robbery. Olga plans to use both to get Chaneeta thrown out of office.

Ancient Secrets September 2008

A novel of Sorcery, jealousy and legends tangles three unlikely adventurers in a drama of treachery. In an effort to return the necklace, stolen from the ancient goddess Ebony before the earth suffers her final blow, the team suffers through the only available path— through the Valley of the Kings laced with trials. Pitted against one they had called friend turned fiend they must cling together to try to save themselves and, if legend is true, the world.

The Pink Lady Slipper October 2005

Trudy Moncha wasn't quite sure what to make of Yachne. Her talk of ghosts, witches and the devil bordered on extreme paranoia, zealot or something worse. Trudy wanted to assure her that she would not harbor evil, but that she was determined to renovate and open The Pink Lady Slipper in the near future. "I had intentions of restoring the Lady Slipper and turning it in to a bed and breakfast." There will be no evil in that. Ordinary families on vacation needing a place to spend the night will find haven at the Lady Slipper. That's what I have planned." She said hoping that appeased Yachne.

Wringing her hands and ready to bolt out the door at the drop of a pin Yachne bubbled over with foreboding. "Oh fine. Another evil den of iniquity. This place needs to be burned. Burned to rid us of its evil," Yachne said agitated, rising to leave. "I must get back. Pastor Joseph will be worried for my well-being."

Bed and Breakfast Murders January 2006

Trapped by a blizzard, no power, heat or telephone contact with the outside world, three murders, and an accident that nearly kills the Wells Fargo agent/guest have Trudy on edge. Then an unexpected wild snowmobile chase that send Trudy Moncha to the hospital to recover from frost bite has her wondering if the serial killer is the one who was chasing her. She is kidnapped from the hospital and held hostage by an insane pair who have their property guarded inside by a trained attack pit bull and outside by his counterpart a Rotweiler of similar intent, ready to tear her apart if she tries to escape, even if she could walk on her severely frost bitten feet. She is determined not to become another murder statistic. Every ounce of self-preservation, courage and ingenuity she can muster becomes her tools for survival.

Watch For The Raven July 2005

There was a ruckus in the marsh ahead. It sounded to him like a big black bear crashing through the woods. Charging straight at him. Josh quickly hunkered down in a mass of scrub oak. The beast charged right at his hiding place, crashing out of the woods storming at him like his tail was a fire. Snorting and puffing, the biggest buck he ever saw leaped over a fallen tree spattering mud and snow straight over Josh's head. An arrow bounced from his left shoulder. It caught on some brush and dropped to the ground. Josh heard footsteps, someone was tracking the deer. Panic held his stomach in its icy grip. He scurried deeper into the brush as he saw the tall Ute Indian.

"They'd as soon scalp a white man as look at him," his friend's words echoed in his head.

Fin, Fur and Fatal February 2010
A patrol car on its nightly rounds slowly passed going in the opposite direction. Garett's mouth went dry. He pulled his hat down tighter, not feeling at all like he'd like to explore what the cops might be looking for on this particular dock. He ticked his hat with his forefinger as a salute to the officers as he passed. Taking a deep breath of relief, he proceeded to drive out of the gate toward the freeway. *Routine drive through,* he repeated trying to convince himself to stay calm, not to look suspicious, not to do anything to attract attention to himself.

Money Isn't Everything May 2010
Money Isn't everything – It isn't love, it isn't security, and it doesn't buy loyalty. It can be a tool, or a murder weapon.

Cauldron July 2010
"Cauldron's name seemed apt. the boiling turmoil that increased daily. *"Who knows what evil lurks in the hearts of men "*—Tiffany knew. With the creaking of that door icy fingered shudders ran the length of her spine. Protection from the undead—the never tamed evil—Everyone knew there was no such thing as vampires?

Antique Armor September 2010
Is it murder, or suicide? Is it a curse on the Antique Armor or something else? Was Aunt Rosa, part of a criminal plot or an unwilling cohort?

Death, Diamonds, And Deceit October 2010
Ewando, South Africa is an enigma. Ex-FBI Agent, now teacher, David Hemingway sees greed and deceit? Do the unexplainable deaths cover the clues he needs? Diamonds, death, deceit, Africa.

Billie A Williams

July Heat, June 2011

What you don't know can't hurt you. "Truth or lies? In the smoldering heat of July, dangerous and unpredictable weather, irrational, unpredictable, and dangerous human behavior explodes Delta's small town peace and tranquility. Can what I know kill me? Judy fears it might

Printed in Great Britain
by Amazon.co.uk, Ltd.,
Marston Gate.